Presented to

_____

With love from

_____

On

_____

ZONDERKIDZ

God's Big Plans for Me Storybook Bible
Copyright © 2017 by Rick Warren

This title is also available as a Zondervan ebook. Visit www.zondervan.com/ebooks.

Requests for information should be addressed to:

Zonderkidz, 3900 Sparks Dr. SE, Grand Rapids, Michigan 49546

ISBN 978-0-310-75039-0

Based on stories from Hurlbut's *The Complete Book of Bible Stories* edited by Jon Walker

Art direction and design: Jody Langley

Printed in China

17 18 19 20 21 22 /DCI/ 22 21 20 19 18 17 16 15 14 13 12 11 10 9 8 7 6 5 4 3 2 1

God's Big Plans *for* Me

STORYBOOK BIBLE
based on the *New York Times* Bestseller
THE PURPOSE DRIVEN LIFE

RICK WARREN

Dedication

This book is dedicated to YOU. Did you know, before you were even born, God had a plan for your life? It's true! That plan is called your purpose— it's what God wants *you* to do here on earth. And, more than anything, God wants you to discover the amazing plan he has for you.

I am grateful for everyone who helped me learn about God's plan. I thank God and you for letting me share what I have learned with you in the pages of this book.

—*Rick Warren*

God decided to choose us long ago in keeping with his plan. He works out everything to fit his plan and purpose.

EPHESIANS 1:11 (NIrV)

What On Earth Am I Here For?

God planned your life long before you came into this world. He put you here on earth for a reason. There are things he wants you to do and a way he wants you to live. That is his plan for you.

How do you know what God's plan is? You can't figure it out by thinking about it. But God will tell you through his Word. The Bible helps us get to know God.

I'm inviting you to go on a special journey with me through the Bible. The Scriptures we will read together will help answer that very big question:

"How does God want me to live my life?"

On our journey, we will read 40 Bible stories. I chose forty because it is an important number in the Bible. Each story will help you understand a little more about God's plan.

I pray this book will bring you the hope and joy that comes when you find out what God put you on this earth to do. I am excited because I know he has planned great things for you.

As you read through the Bible stories, I pray they will help you become the person God created you to be.

Let's get started together!

Table of Contents

It All Starts with God

Day 1

This book is for you, but it's not about you. It's about God! Because God is the one who made everything—from sunsets and stars to storms and seasons. Without God, there would be nothing.

You can learn a lot about God just by looking at the world around you. It shows you how awesome he is. And remember to look at yourself too. You're a very special part of God's creation.

As you read this story from the Bible, remember that God was there at the very beginning. He planned something big and important for all of creation, and that includes you!

Creation

GENESIS 1:1–2:2

In the beginning—a long, long time ago—God created the earth, sun, moon, and stars. But before anything was created, there was God. God has always been!

Then God spoke, and the earth and heavens came into being. The earth was blacker than the sky at midnight. God said, "Let there be light," and the light came shining bright into the world. God called the light "day," and he called the dark "night." That was the first day on Earth.

Next, God told all the dark clouds around the earth to break up. The sky became visible. God called the sky over the earth "heaven." The night and the morning made the second day.

8

9

"Let the water on the earth come together in one place, and let the dry land rise up," God said. And that's what happened.

God called the water "sea," and he named the dry land "earth." Then he filled the earth with grass, flowers, and fruit trees. This was the third day on Earth.

God said, "Let there be lights in the huge space of the sky." The sun began to shine during the day, and the moon and stars began to shine at night. This happened on the fourth day.

On the fifth day, God said, "Let fish swim in the sea and birds fly in the air." So fish flapped their fins and began to swim in the sea, and birds waved their wings and flew over the land.

Then God said on the sixth day, "Let there be animals on the earth." And all kinds of animals crawled through the grass and ran over the ground and soared in the skies and floated in the seas.

In six days God made the heavens, the earth, and everything that's in them. But he wasn't finished. His greatest creation was yet to come.

12

It All Starts with God

Think

God has an important plan for everything he created.

Question

When you go outside, what are some of the things you see that God created?

Remember

"In the beginning, God created the heavens and the earth."

Genesis 1:1

13

You Make God Happy

You are a child of God. The moment you were born, God celebrated and welcomed you into the world. God smiles when he thinks of you because he loves you so much! You make God happy— and that's why you were created.

That's why God made Adam and Eve too.

Day 2

14

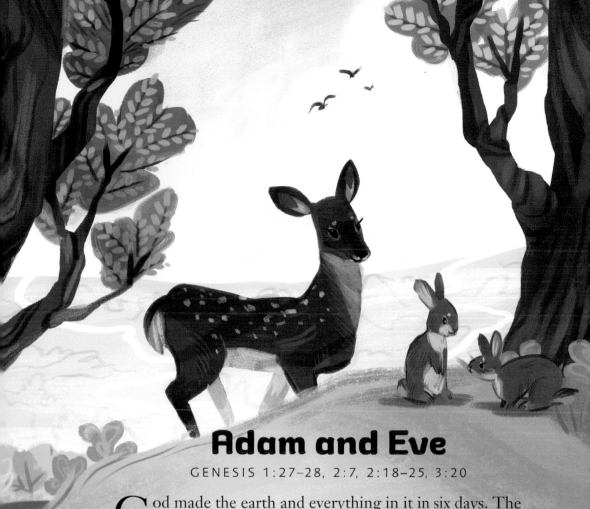

Adam and Eve

GENESIS 1:27–28, 2:7, 2:18–25, 3:20

God made the earth and everything in it in six days. The world was now ready for men and women to enjoy it. God said, "I will make a man, but he's going to be different from all the other animals. He will stand up, he will be able to feel emotion, and he will be in charge of the earth and everything that's in it."

God took some dust from the ground and made a man and breathed life into him. The man came alive and stood up. Then God named the first man Adam.

When Adam went to sleep, God took a rib from his side and from that rib made a woman. He brought her to Adam, and Adam named her Eve. Adam and Eve loved each other. They were happy in the home God had given them, and God was happy he had made them.

You Make God Happy

Think

If I was created to make God happy, I must be very important to God.

Remember

"God said, 'It is not good for the man to be alone. I will make a helper who is just right for him.'"

Genesis 2:18

Question

What are the things you do that please God? Does pleasing God make you happy too?

God Trusts You

God gives us many gifts. Have you thought about how much he has given you? Think about the beautiful things in nature, the people who love you, and all the special things you are able to do. God has given you all these wonderful things because he trusts you.

The earth isn't ours; it belongs to God. But he needs us to take care of it. Did you know the very first job God gave humans was to take care of his stuff on Earth? He gave that job to Adam and Eve. While you are here on Earth, it's your job too.

Day 3

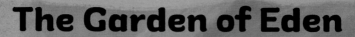

The Garden of Eden

GENESIS 2:8–20

God wasn't through when he created Adam and Eve. He made a beautiful garden called the Garden of Eden. It stretched for miles and miles in every direction and had four rivers. God planted trees and made the grass grow and the flowers bloom. It was Paradise!

God gave the garden to the man and told him to gather fruit from the trees and plants from the ground for food. Then God brought all the animals to Adam and asked him to name them. Now it was Adam's job to take care of the earth and the animals in the garden.

For a long time Adam and Eve were at peace in their beautiful garden. They didn't even know what evil or sin was. They did what God asked, and they talked with him just as we would talk to a friend.

God Trusts You

Think
God trusts me to take care of all that he gives me.

Remember
"The LORD God put the man in the Garden of Eden. He put him there to farm its land and take care of it."

Genesis 2:15

Question
What has God given you that he wants you to take care of?

21

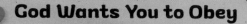

God Wants You to Obey

Day 4

Every day, God gives you tests so that you can become a better person. He wants to see how you treat others, if you follow the rules, and how you handle big disappointments and problems. The good news is God wants you to pass the tests. And if you need his help, all you have to do is ask.

Adam and Eve failed a very big test because they didn't obey God. But even though they were forced to leave their beautiful garden, God never stopped loving them. And he never stops loving you!

When the World Changed

GENESIS 2:16–17, 3:1–24

For a long time Adam and Eve were at peace in their beautiful garden called Eden. But because it was important for Adam and Eve to understand obedience, God said to them, "You may eat the fruit of all the trees in the garden except one. Do not touch the one in the middle of the garden. If you eat the fruit from that tree, you will die."

There was a snake living in the garden. One day this snake said to Eve, "Did God really say that you must not eat the fruit from that special tree in the middle of the garden?"

Eve answered, "If we eat the fruit of that tree, God says we will die."

23

Then the snake said, "You will not die! God knows that if you eat the fruit of that tree, you will become as wise as he is. Then you will know what is good and what is evil." The snake was lying to Eve and trying to get her to disobey God. Eve looked at the tree and thought how good the fruit would taste. Then she ate the fruit and gave some to Adam. He ate it too.

For the first time in their lives Adam and Eve were afraid, because they knew they had done wrong. They tried to hide from God among the trees of the garden.

But God found them. Because Adam and Eve had disobeyed God, they were forced to leave their beautiful home in the Garden of Eden. They were never allowed to return.

26

God Wants You to Obey

Think
God wants me to pass life's tests.

Question
What is one test God has given you? Did you pass his test?

Remember
"Have respect for God and obey his commandments. This is what he expects of all human beings."
Ecclesiastes 12:13

27

What Makes God Smile?

Learning to love God and be loved by him is the most important thing of all. Why? Because it makes God happy! God made you so he could love you, and he smiles when you love him back. What else makes God smile? When you trust that he knows what's best for you and obey him with your whole heart.

In the story below, Noah loved God more than anything else in the world. He trusted God even when it didn't make sense—like when there was no rain when God told him to build the giant boat!

Day 5

Noah and the Ark

GENESIS 6–9

Adam and Eve's children had a lot of children, and their children had a lot of children. The earth was filled with people, but God saw how bad they had become and how they thought about evil all the time. Then God looked all over the earth and saw one good man. The man's name was Noah.

God told Noah, "I'm going to put an end to all people. But you and your family will be saved because you tried to do what is right." Then God told Noah to build a very large boat called an "ark" because he was going to bring a great flood to the earth.

It probably seemed pretty strange to all of Noah's neighbors when he started building a big boat when there was no rain in sight or a lake or any water for it to float on. But Noah did what God told him to do because he trusted God to take care of him. It didn't matter what other people thought of him. It didn't matter that no one else loved God like Noah did. When people trust God like that, it makes him smile!

Finally the ark was finished, and Noah and his family went inside. Then God brought all the animals and birds of the earth to the ark, and they went inside too.

31

In a few days, the rain began to fall. It kept falling until the water was so deep it covered the whole earth. It rained for forty days!

When it stopped raining and the water had dried up, Noah opened the door of the ark, and his whole family and the animals and birds came out and stood on dry ground. The first thing Noah did was give thanks to God for saving his family. God was happy with Noah and made a promise that he would never flood the earth again. A rainbow appeared in the sky as a sign of God's promise.

What Makes God Smile?

Think
God smiles when I trust him to do what is best for me.

Remember
"The LORD takes delight in those who have respect for him. They put their hope in his faithful love."

Psalm 147:11

Question
Trusting God doesn't always make sense, but God wants you to do it anyway. What is one thing you can trust God to handle?

God Wants to Be Your Friend

Day 6

Did you know that God wants to be your friend? He wants you to get to know him, and you do that by talking to him. You can say anything to God, and you never have to pretend. You can tell him exactly how you feel, because he just wants you to be yourself.

Abram was God's friend. When the Lord came to visit, Abram offered him food to eat, water to wash his feet, and a tree to rest under. He cared for his friend, and God showed him that all things are possible when you have God as your friend.

God's Promise to Abram

GENESIS 17, 18:1–15, 21:1–7

The Lord saw that Abram was good and faithful, so he told him, "Gather together all your family, and leave this country. I will show you a place to go where I will make you into a great nation and bless you."

36

Abram didn't really understand what God meant, but he obeyed God. He took his wife, their family, his flocks of sheep and herds of cattle, and his servants. After a long journey, Abram and his family came into the land of Canaan.

The Lord came to Abram again and said, "I will be with you and your children forever." But Abram was confused. He didn't have any children! He had a large family around him and many servants, but he didn't have a son. Now he was an old man and his wife, Sarai, was also old.

That night God told Abram to look up at the sky and count the stars. Do you think he could count them all? No! There are way too many stars for anyone to count! God told Abram, "Your children and their children in years to come will be more than all the stars that you can see." Wow! That's a lot of family that God promised Abram.

Abram did not see how God could keep his promise, but he believed what God said. God promised to give Abram a son and to give the people a land, and Abram promised to serve God faithfully. That kind of promise is called a "covenant."

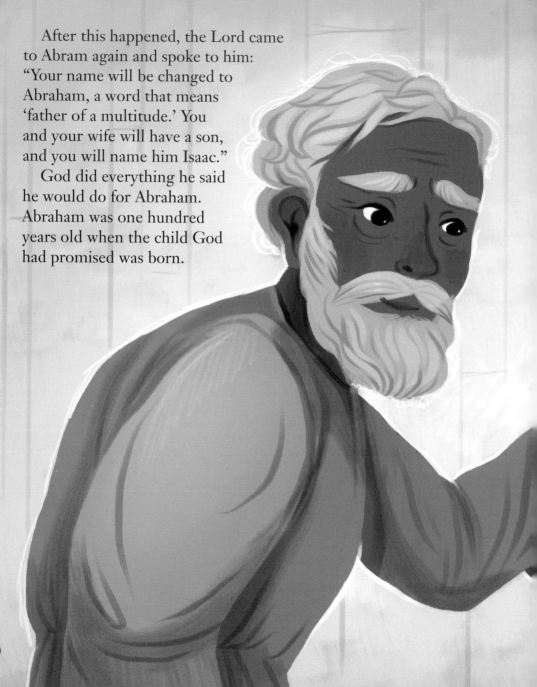

After this happened, the Lord came to Abram again and spoke to him: "Your name will be changed to Abraham, a word that means 'father of a multitude.' You and your wife will have a son, and you will name him Isaac."

God did everything he said he would do for Abraham. Abraham was one hundred years old when the child God had promised was born.

God Wants to Be Your Friend

Think
There is nothing more important than becoming God's friend.

Remember
"Come near to God, and he will come near to you."
James 4:8

Question
Think about how you talk to your best friend. Do you talk to God the same way?

41

Living in Peace with Others

God wants us to learn how to get along with each other. Sometimes that's easy, but sometimes it's really hard. As we share our lives with others, we don't always agree, and we make mistakes. We hurt each other. But God forgives us, and he wants us to forgive others.

Esau and Jacob were brothers who were very different. They didn't get along at all. Jacob tricked his brother. Do you think Esau could forgive his brother's big mistake?

Esau and Jacob

GENESIS 25–33

Isaac and his wife Rebekah had twin sons, Esau and Jacob. Esau loved to hunt, but Jacob liked to stay home and care for his father's flocks of animals. Isaac loved Esau more because Esau always brought his father delicious meat from the animals he killed when hunting. But Rebekah loved Jacob because she saw that he was wise and careful in his work.

After a long time, Isaac became very old and weak and so blind that he could barely see. He said to Esau, "My son, I'm very old, but before I die, I want to give you God's blessing. Make me some of your delicious meat. After I've eaten, I will give you the blessing."

Esau went out in the field to hunt. But Rebekah was listening to what Isaac said. Because she loved Jacob more than Esau, she wanted Jacob to have the blessing.

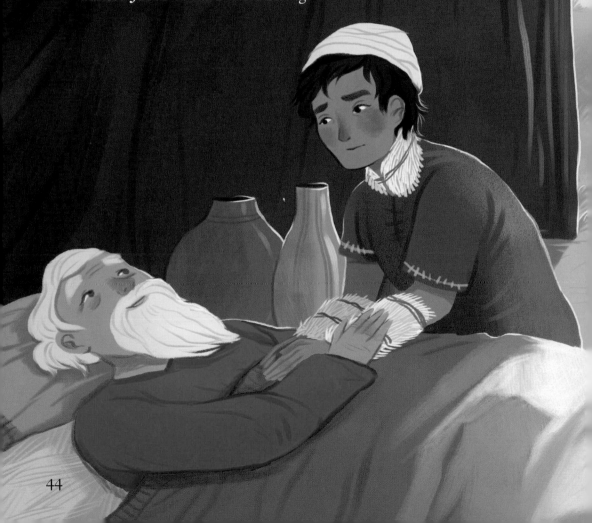

Rebekah prepared meat just like Esau cooked for his father and dressed Jacob in Esau's clothes. She placed skins from the goats on his hands and neck so they would feel rough and hairy like Esau.

Jacob took the dinner to his father. Isaac fell for Jacob's lie and gave him the blessing.

When Esau came in from hunting and Isaac realized who he was, he told him, "I have already blessed Jacob! There is nothing left for me to give to you."

Esau knew Jacob had cheated him, and he was really angry. In fact, he hated Jacob! Jacob left their home because he was afraid of what Esau would do to him.

The brothers didn't see each other
again until years later. With God's help,
they were able to forgive each other.

Living in Peace with Others

Think
God is happy when
I get along with
others.

Remember
"If possible, live in peace
with everyone. Do that
as much as you can."
Romans 12:18

Question
Who is someone that
you need to get along
with better?

47

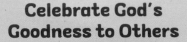

Celebrate God's Goodness to Others

Do you sometimes feel like God gave someone else a lot more than he gave you? Just remember: God knows what he's doing, and he wants you to trust him. When he gives good things to others, he wants you to be happy for them. Joseph's father gave him a special gift to show his love— a beautiful, colorful coat. That made Joseph's brothers jealous. They didn't trust that all the things they didn't understand and didn't like about Joseph were part of God's plan.

Joseph and His Brothers

GENESIS 37, 39:1–5

Jacob had twelve sons, but he loved Joseph best. He made a beautiful coat of many colors and gave it to Joseph to show him how much he loved him. It made the older brothers really jealous!

The brothers were also jealous because of Joseph's strange dreams. They thought the dreams meant they were supposed to bow down to Joseph, and they definitely weren't going to do that.

One day, Joseph's older brothers were taking care of their father's sheep in a town far away. Jacob sent Joseph to check on them. When the brothers saw Joseph coming in his bright coat, they said, "Look, the dreamer is coming! Let's throw him into a pit. Then we can tell Father that some wild animal ate him."

The brothers grabbed Joseph, tore off his robe, and tossed him in a pit. They decided to sell Joseph as a slave to some traders who were on their way to Egypt.

51

In Egypt, Joseph worked hard and became an important servant. One day, the pharaoh had Joseph brought to him. He had had strange dreams, and he wanted Joseph to tell him what they meant. Joseph was able to help Pharaoh because God was with him. This made Pharaoh very happy and he wanted to reward Joseph.

Pharaoh made Joseph ruler over the land of Egypt. Joseph made sure the Egyptian people had enough food to eat. Joseph's father sent his brothers to Egypt to buy grain because they didn't have enough food to eat when a famine came. They went to Joseph to ask for food, but they didn't even recognize him!

But Joseph recognized his brothers and forgave them for what they had done. He and his brothers hugged and cried together.

The brothers went home with good news and lots of food. Joseph sent wagons with them to use to bring his father and his family back to Egypt. They were all happy together for many years.

Celebrate
God's Goodness
to Others

Think
I am thankful for who
I am and what I have.

Question
Instead of wishing you had what
someone else has, you can stop
and be thankful for what God
has given you. What is something
God has given you that you can
be thankful for?

Remember
"Love is patient.
Love is kind. It does
not want what
belongs to others."
I Corinthians 13:4

55

God Has Big Plans for You

God was thinking of you even before he made the world. God chose the color of your skin, your hair, and your eyes, and he chose your special skills and talents. He decided when and where you would be born and who your parents would be. He planned everything about you.

And God planned everything about Moses. He knew everything about Moses and everything that would happen to him before he was born.

The Hidden Baby

EXODUS 1:1–2:11

After Joseph died, a new pharaoh became ruler. He saw that there were a lot of Israelite people in Egypt. That made the new pharaoh nervous, so he made them become slaves.

But the Israelite people just kept growing! So Pharaoh ordered that all boy babies born to Israelite families had to be thrown into the Nile River. Only baby girls would be allowed to live.

One mother hid her boy baby for three months after he was born. But she couldn't hide him forever, so she thought up a plan to save his life.

She got a small basket and covered it with tar to keep water out. Then she put her baby in the basket and put the basket in the river.

The baby's sister, Miriam, followed the basket as it floated in
the water to see what would happen to her brother.

When Pharaoh's daughter came to the river to bathe, she saw
the basket floating in the water. The princess found the baby
inside. She decided to keep him and raise him in the palace.

Miriam came out of her hiding place and offered to help.
"Should I go find someone to take care of the baby for you?" she
asked.

The princess said, "Yes," so Miriam ran as fast as she could and
brought her mother to the princess. The mother must have been
so glad to take care of her own baby again! No one could harm
him now that the princess of Egypt protected him.

When he was old enough to leave his mother, Pharaoh's daughter named the child Moses and took him into the palace. Even before Moses was born, God knew all these things would happen and that he had big plans for Moses.

God Has Big Plans for You

Think
Before he made the world, God thought of me.

Remember
"Your eyes saw my body even before it was formed."
Psalm 139:16

Question
What special things can you do? What are your talents?

You Were Made to Serve God

You are one of a kind. God planned exactly how he wanted you to serve him, and then he made you in a special way so that you have just what you need to do what God wants you to do. The things you do matter and the things that happen to you matter. God uses all of it to shape you to serve him and other people.

God created Moses to serve him by leading his people out of Egypt. Moses thought God chose the wrong person. But God never makes mistakes!

God Calls Moses

EXODUS 3–4

Moses lived in the palace as a prince of Egypt for a long time. But later the Egyptians became his enemies, so he left the palace and became a shepherd. One day, while Moses was feeding his sheep, he saw a bush that looked like it was on fire. But the bush wasn't burning up.

As Moses walked closer, he heard a voice coming out of the bush, saying, "Moses, Moses!"

Would that scare you? I bet it scared Moses, but he said, "Here I am."

The voice from the bush said, "I am God. I have seen my people hurting in Egypt. I am going to set them free from the Egyptians and take them to their own land. You will lead my people out of Egypt."

63

Moses thought for sure he wasn't the right person for the job, but God told him he would be with Moses and help him. God told Moses, "Go to Pharaoh and tell him to let my people go. At first Pharaoh will not let them go. But I will show my power in Egypt, and then he will let you leave."

Moses wanted to make sure everyone would
believe God had sent him. God told Moses to
take the wooden rod in his hand and throw
it on the ground. Moses threw it, and
the staff turned into a snake!
When Moses picked it up, the
snake turned back into a stick.
God told Moses to show the
people this amazing thing
as a sign that God was
with him.

Moses obeyed God and did what God told him to
do. God used Moses to lead his people to freedom!

You Were Made to Serve God

Think

Before God made me, he decided what he wanted me to do on Earth.

Remember

"Before I formed you in your mother's body I chose you. Before you were born I set you apart to serve me."

Jeremiah 1:5

Question

What do you love to do? How can it help others?

67

The Glory of God

What is the glory of God? It is who God is. It is his nature, his importance, his splendor, and his power. You can see God's glory in everything from the tiniest form of life to the huge Milky Way galaxy because they all show how big and wide and creative God's love is. You can see God's glory in yourself! But you can't add anything to his glory—just like you can't make the sun shine brighter.

God is very powerful. That is part of his glory. It is part of who he is, and he shows his power and glory through Moses in this story.

Miracle at the Red Sea

EXODUS 13:17–15:1

When the children of Israel (they are also called the Hebrew people) marched out of Egypt, they started toward the land of Canaan. God went with the people as they walked. In the daytime he led them by a great cloud that looked like a tall pillar. At night the pillar turned into fire so everyone could see it and follow. Whenever the pillar stopped, the people knew it was time to rest.

The Hebrew people were surprised to see the pillar turn right toward the Red Sea instead of going around it. When it stopped for them to rest, there was a sea full of water in front of them, mountains on each side of them, and soon they heard the sound of horses and chariots behind them.

After the children of Israel left Egypt, Pharaoh decided to march out after them with his army. He wanted to bring them back, to go on working as slaves. When the Hebrew people saw the army, they were terrified!

"Don't be afraid!" Moses cried. "Watch and see how God will save you."

God told Moses to hold out his wooden rod over the Red Sea. When Moses obeyed, the water split apart to leave a path of dry sand through the middle of the sea. The people of Israel went through the sea on dry ground, with a wall of water on both sides of their path.

71

When the Egyptians tried to
follow the Hebrews, their chariot
wheels sank into the sand and
broke off. "The Lord is fighting
for them!" Pharaoh's army cried.
"Let's run away!"

73

When the Hebrews reached the other side of the sea, Moses lifted his hand and the walls of water closed together. Water covered the Egyptian army. No one was left to chase the children of Israel.

Moses and his people knew that God had saved them. They danced and sang a song of victory!

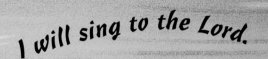

I will sing to the Lord.

He has triumphed gloriously.

The Glory of God

Think

Everything around me shows God's glory, including me.

Remember ✏️

"The heavens tell about the glory of God. The skies show that his hands created them."

Psalm 19:1

Question ❓

What is something that has happened in your life that shows how big and powerful God is?

75

It's All About Love

Life is all about love. That's because God is love! Learning how to love God and love other people is the most important lesson you can learn. You show others that you love them by giving them your time and your help.

In today's story, Naomi wanted to go home to Israel after her husband and two sons died. But her daughter-in-law, Ruth, loved her with all her heart and would not let her go alone. She stayed by her side and worked hard to make sure Naomi would be cared for.

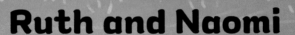

Ruth and Naomi

RUTH 1–4

Naomi was a Hebrew woman who lived in Moab. Her husband and two sons died, and she and her daughters-in-law, Ruth and Orpah, were very sad.

Naomi decided to go back to Israel to live near her family. Naomi told Ruth and Orpah, "My daughters, go back to your mothers' homes. May God bless each of you with a new husband and a happy home."

Orpah went back to her parents' home. But Ruth wanted to stay with Naomi and take care of her. She said, "Do not ask me to leave you. Wherever you go, I will go too."

Naomi and Ruth traveled to Israel. All of Naomi's relatives were very happy to see her again. One of Naomi's relatives was a very rich man named Boaz. He owned large fields and grew a lot of grain. Ruth went to the fields of Boaz to pick up the extra grain his workers dropped so that she and Naomi could eat.

One day, Boaz saw her there and found out who she was. He
went to Ruth and said, "Don't go to any other field to gather
grain. No one will harm you here." Boaz also shared some of his
food with Ruth at mealtime. Ruth and Naomi were thankful and
happy that Boaz showed them kindness.

Soon Boaz and Ruth were married. Ruth chose Boaz because he was kind, and Boaz loved Ruth because she was kind and took care of Naomi. They both knew that was important to God.

Ruth and Boaz had a son named Obed. When he grew up, Obed became the father of Jesse. And Jesse was the father of David, the shepherd boy who became king of all Israel.

It's All About Love

Think

Life is all about loving God and loving others.

Remember ✏️

"The way we show our love is to obey God's commands. He commands you to lead a life of love."

2 John 1:6

Question ❓

How can you show people that you love them?

God Made You to be YOU

You bring glory to God when you follow his plan for you. It allows people to see God's greatness when you do what he created you to do. When anything in creation follows God's plan, it brings glory to God. Birds bring glory to God by flying, chirping, nesting, and doing other bird-like things. Even a tiny ant brings glory to God just by being itself and doing what God created it to do.

God had a plan for Samuel. He created Samuel to be a prophet (someone who delivers a message from God). When Hannah and Samuel followed God's plan, they brought glory to God.

God Calls Samuel

1 SAMUEL 1, 3

A woman named Hannah went to worship at the tabernacle. She needed God's help, so she prayed a special prayer: "Lord, if you hear me and give me a son, I will give him back to you to serve you as long as he lives."

The Lord heard Hannah's prayer and gave her a little boy. She named him Samuel. Hannah knew God had answered her prayer and given her the baby.

Hannah kept her promise to God, and when Samuel was still very young, she brought him to Eli the priest. Samuel stayed with Eli and worked in the tabernacle. He lit candles, opened doors, and helped Eli.

83

One night, Samuel heard a voice calling him. He thought it was Eli speaking to him, so he got up from his bed and ran to him. He asked Eli, "What do you want me to do?"

Eli answered, "I didn't call you. Go back to bed."

Samuel lay down in bed, but he soon heard the voice calling again, "Samuel! Samuel!"

Samuel went to Eli again, and Eli told him the same thing.

The third time Samuel showed up, Eli realized the voice calling Samuel belonged to God. He told Samuel, "Go lie down. If the voice speaks to you again, say 'Speak, Lord. Your servant is listening.'"

Samuel obeyed Eli. The voice really was God! When Samuel told Eli everything that God had said, Eli knew Samuel was the person God had chosen to speak to Israel.

When he grew up, Samuel went to the people of Israel to teach them to obey and love God. And while the people followed Samuel, they had peace.

God Made You to be YOU

Think

God made me to be me, and when I am, I show others God's greatness.

Remember

"All things are for his praise. May God be given the glory forever!"

Romans 11:36

Question

How did God create you to be different from everyone else?

Day 14

Trusting God is Worship

Trusting God means believing that he knows what is best for you. You expect him to help you with problems and even do things that seem impossible to you. When you trust God, you are worshiping him, and that makes God happy. To worship God means to show him you love and respect him.

When David faced Goliath for the fight of his life, he didn't trust in his own strength. He trusted in God's strength! He expected God to help him.

David Beats a Giant

1 SAMUEL 17

When Saul was king, Israel was at war with the Philistine people. One day, a shepherd named David went to visit his brothers in their army camp. While he was there, a giant man named Goliath came out of the Philistine camp. He was nine feet tall and wore bronze armor from his head to his feet.

Goliath called out across the valley, "Choose one of your men to come and fight with me. If he can kill me, we will become your slaves. If I kill him, you will become our slaves!"

The giant had been coming to the valley and shouting these words at the Israelites for forty days, but no one had been brave enough to go down and fight him. David couldn't believe it. He told everyone, "If no one else will do it, I'll fight Goliath."

89

David was not afraid. He trusted God to keep him safe. He gathered five smooth stones and went to face Goliath with his sling and his staff (a long stick).

Goliath was angry when he saw who had come out to fight him. "What is this? You must think I'm a dog to send a boy with a stick to fight me!"

David answered, "You come against me with a sword and a spear, but I come to you in the name of the God of the whole earth."

Then David took out his sling and hurled a stone at Goliath. David's aim was good, and his stone struck the Philistine right in the forehead! The giant fell down to the ground like a tall tree.

When the Philistines saw this, they turned and ran back to their homes. David won a great battle that day. He worshiped God by believing God would help him win the fight with Goliath.

Trusting God Is Worship

Think
God smiles when
I trust him.

Remember
"This day the LORD will give
me the victory over you."
I Samuel 17:46

Question
How can you
show God that
you trust him?

What God Cares About Most

A friend cares about what is important to the other person. When you are friends with God, you care about the things he cares about and you're happy about the things that make him happy.

What do you think God cares about most? He cares about the people around you who aren't friends with him yet. And he wants you to tell those people about him.

Solomon could have asked God for anything. He could have asked for money or fame or fancy things. But Solomon asked God for something else, and it made God happy.

Solomon Asks for Wisdom

1 KINGS 3:3–15, 4:29–34

Solomon was just a young man when he became king. He worshiped and obeyed the Lord. One night, God came to Solomon in a dream and spoke to him: "Ask me for anything you want, and I will give it to you."

Solomon thought about it and then said, "Lord, you have made me king in this place while I am still so young. Will you give me wisdom and knowledge so that I can make good decisions and rule in the right way?"

97

God was happy with Solomon's choice. He said, "You didn't ask for a long life or lots of money or power. You have asked for wisdom, so I will give you more wisdom than any king who has lived or will ever live."

In fact, God was so pleased with Solomon's request that he told him he would also give him the things he didn't ask for, like honor and riches. He promised Solomon that if he obeyed God always, God would let him live and be king for a very long time.

Then Solomon woke up and knew that he had been dreaming. But it was a dream that came true! God gave Solomon all he had promised.

What God Cares About Most

Think

What God thinks is important should also be important to me.

Remember

"If any of you needs wisdom, you should ask God for it. He will give it to you."

James 1:5

Question

What can you ask God for to help you tell other people about him?

God Wants You to Share Your Life

God wants us to share our lives with other people, and that's called fellowship. Fellowship happens when we give to others and they give to us. It means we share and listen and serve and comfort each other. To have real fellowship, you need to do two things: Be honest about who you are, and think more of others than yourself.

Esther does both of those things in this story, and she is able to help her people when they need her most.

Esther Saves Her People

ESTHER 3–5, 7–8

King Xerxes made Esther the new queen of Persia, and he loved her very much. But Esther's cousin Mordecai told her not to tell anyone that she was Jewish because some of the people in the palace hated the Jews.

Haman

Everyone in the palace had to bow down to a man named Haman because he was a friend of the king. But Mordecai would only worship and bow down to God. This made Haman very angry. Haman went to the king and asked that Mordecai and all the Jewish people in the land be killed.

Haman was a smooth talker. When he told the king the Jews were dangerous, the king believed him. He told Haman he could do whatever he wanted with the Jews. Remember—no one knew that Queen Esther was a Jew.

But Mordecai heard about Haman's plan to kill all the Jews in Persia. He sent a message to Queen Esther: She must go to the king and beg for help for her people. Esther was afraid, but Mordecai told her, "Maybe the whole reason God brought you to the palace is to save your people."

So Esther bravely went to see the king. She invited King Xerxes and Haman to a banquet.

"What do you want, Queen Esther?" the king asked at the banquet. "I will give you anything."

"I want you to save my life and the lives of my people!" Esther said. Then Esther explained Haman's terrible plan to kill all the Jews.

The king was angry Haman had tricked him, and he ordered that Haman be killed.

Esther's courage saved the day! Mordecai and the Jewish people were safe because Esther cared for them so much.

God Wants You to Share Your Life

Think
I need other people in my life.

Remember ✏️
"Carry one another's heavy loads."
Galatians 6:2

Question ❓
You're probably good at sharing your toys and games and belongings. What are some other ways you can share with others?

105

Worshiping God

There are so many ways to worship God. You can worship him by enjoying being outside or by listening to beautiful music. You can worship him all by yourself or in a room full of people. An amazing thing happens when we worship God: Our own hearts are filled with joy!

This is a psalm that David wrote. He wanted the whole world to worship God—even the stars and the mountains! To praise God means to celebrate how great he is.

One way you can worship God is to read the Bible out loud and believe in your heart what it says.

Day 17

Praise the Lord

PSALM 148:1–4, 7–14

Praise the LORD.
Praise the LORD from the heavens.
Praise him in the heavens above.
Praise him, all his angels.
Praise him, all his angels in heaven.

Praise him, sun and moon.
Praise him, all you shining stars.
Praise him, you highest heavens.
Praise him, you waters above the skies.
Praise the LORD from the earth,
    you great sea creatures and all the
    deepest parts of the ocean.

Praise him, lightning and hail, snow and clouds.
Praise him, you stormy winds that obey him.
Praise him, all you mountains and hills.
Praise him, all you fruit trees and cedar trees.
Praise him, all you wild animals and cattle.
Praise him, you small creatures and
    flying birds.

Praise him, you kings of the earth and all nations.
Praise him, all you princes and rulers on earth.
Praise him, young men and women.
Praise him, old men and children.
Let them praise the name of the LORD.

His name alone is honored.
His glory is higher than the earth and the heavens.
He has given his people a strong king.
All his faithful people praise him for that gift.
All the people of Israel are close to his heart.
Praise the LORD.

Worshiping God

Think
When I praise God,
it makes him happy.

Remember
"Praise him, young men and
women. Praise him, old men
and children. Let them praise
the name of the LORD."
Psalm 148:12–13

Question
What are
some ways
that you can
worship God?

God Wants All of You

God doesn't want just little bits of your life. He asks for all your heart, all your soul, all your mind, and all your strength. He wants all of your love and worship. Remember, to worship God means to show him you love and respect him.

But sometimes we worship the wrong things, like famous people or fancy toys or sports teams. You can't do that and follow God's plan. He wants all of you!

King Nebuchadnezzar ordered everyone in his kingdom to worship gold—or else! But three men bravely said, "No!" All of their worship was for God alone.

The Fiery Furnace

DANIEL 3:8–30

The King of Persia, Nebuchadnezzar, had a golden statue made. It was almost a hundred feet high and could be seen from far away. When it was finished, the king called everyone to come to a big service and worship it.

But three Hebrew friends—Shadrach, Meshach, and Abednego—would not bow down to the statue. They worshiped only the one true God. They knew statues were not the real God.

When King Nebuchadnezzar found out the three friends refused to worship his statue, he was very angry. "Throw those men into the furnace of fire!" he shouted.

But the three men were not afraid. They said, "The God we serve can save us if that's what he wants. But even if God doesn't save us, we will never worship the king's statue or any false god that you make."

The king became even angrier. He told his servants to make the furnace seven times hotter than usual. Then Shadrach, Meshach, and Abednego were tied up and thrown in the fire.

But when King Nebuchadnezzar looked in the furnace door, he could not believe what he saw. There were *four men* walking around inside! And one of them looked like an angel.

The king called to the three men, "Shadrach, Meshach, and Abednego, servants of the Most High God! Come out of the fire!"

They came out and stood before the king. Everyone could see they were alive and well. Not one hair on their heads had been burned. They didn't even smell like smoke!

The king told everyone, "The God of these men is amazing! He sent an angel and saved their lives. There is no other God who can save his people like this!"

God Wants All of You

Think

God wants me to worship only him.

Remember

"Love the Lord your God with all your heart and with all your soul. Love him with all your mind and with all your strength."

Mark 12:30

Question

What is something besides God that you sometimes worship?

115

Say "Yes!" to God

God is working all the time, in every person's life, and he wants you to be a part of his big plan for the world. He has a job for you to do, but he wants to be in charge because he knows what is best. He asks you to trust and obey him. He wants you to say, "Yes, Lord!" to whatever he asks you to do.

Mary obeyed God gladly. She knew God would do a miracle, even though she didn't know how it would happen. She didn't understand, but she trusted that God had all the answers.

An Angel Visits Mary

LUKE 1:26–45

One day, God sent an angel named Gabriel to the city of Nazareth. Gabriel went to a young girl named Mary and said, "You have been chosen by God! The Lord is with you."

This surprised Mary. So the angel said, "Do not be afraid, Mary. God is very happy with you. You will give birth to a son. You must name him Jesus because he will save people from their sins. He will be great and will be called the Son of God. The Lord will make him a king, and he will rule forever over his people."

Mary could not understand how all this would happen. She was engaged to Joseph, but she wasn't married yet. Then the angel said, "God's power will make this possible."

Mary was still a little scared but said, "I serve the Lord." She trusted God knew what was best for her and that he would take care of her. Mary said "Yes!" to God.

Say "Yes!" to God

Think
God wants me to say "Yes!" to whatever he tells me to do.

Remember
"If you love me, obey my commands."
John 14:15

Question
What is something God has told you to do? Have you said "Yes!" to God?

119

The Reason for Everything

It's all for God! The universe is here to show the glory of God. It is the reason for everything that exists, including you. And God's glory is best seen in Jesus Christ.

He is the Light of the World. Because of Jesus, we are no longer in the dark about what God is really like. Jesus came to Earth so we could fully understand God's loving character.

Day 20

God's Son Comes to Earth

LUKE 2:1–20

Soon after Mary and Joseph were married in Nazareth, the emperor decided he wanted to count all his people. He commanded everyone to go to the city their family had come from. Mary and Joseph traveled to Bethlehem and it was almost time for Mary's baby to be born!

When they got to Bethlehem, there was no place for them to stay. The only place they could find to spend the night was a stable. That night, their little baby was born. Mary wrapped him in soft cloths. For his bed, she laid him in a box called a manger, where the animals were fed.

The same night some shepherds were watching over their sheep in a field near Bethlehem. Suddenly a bright light shone down from heaven, and they saw a shining angel standing before them. They were scared, but the angel said, "Do not be afraid! I bring you good news that is for all people! Today in Bethlehem a Savior has been born. He is Christ the Lord! You will find him wrapped in soft cloths and lying in a manger."

Suddenly the sky above them was full of angels. They were praising God and singing, "Glory to God!"

The shepherds could hardly believe their eyes. They said to each other, "Let's go to Bethlehem and see this child that we heard about."

The shepherds ran to Bethlehem as fast as they could and found the new baby in a manger, just like the angel had said. When they left, they told everyone about what God had done. Everyone who heard their story was amazed.

The Reason for Everything

Think
Jesus is the reason for everything.

Remember
"Do not be afraid. I bring you good news. It will bring great joy for all the people. Today in the town of David a Savior has been born to you. He is the Messiah, the Lord."
Luke 2:10–11

Question
How does Jesus help you understand God's character?

Made for a Mission

There are five big things God wants you to do on Earth. He wants you to (1) love him, (2) be a part of his family, (3) become like him, (4) serve him, and (5) tell others about him. God wants you to be a messenger of his love to the world! He wants all of his children to do these five things, but he made you in a specific way so you can use your gifts and talents to complete your mission.

Even when Jesus was a boy, he clearly understood he was made for a mission.

The Boy Jesus Amazes the Scholars

LUKE 2:41–52

Every spring Jews from all parts of the country went to the great city of Jerusalem to worship during the feast called Passover. When he was twelve, Jesus went with his family to this huge Passover feast. For the first time, he walked through the courts of the temple and saw its altar. He saw the priests in their white robes and the Levites blowing silver trumpets.

Jesus was only a boy, but he felt how special this place was. He knew he was the Son of God, and he knew this house belonged to his heavenly Father. His heart was filled with the beauty of worship in the temple.

When it was time for his family to go home to Nazareth, Jesus was somehow left behind. At first no one noticed he was missing. There were so many people traveling together in one big group. Everyone thought he must be there somewhere. But night came, and Jesus could not be found.

His parents, Mary and Joseph, were very afraid for their son. They left their group and hurried back to Jerusalem to look for him. They searched everywhere they could think of, but they couldn't find him. Finally, on the third day, they went back to the temple.

There was Jesus, sitting with a group of teachers of the Jewish law. He had been listening to their words and asking them questions.

Mary said to him, "Jesus, why have you treated us this way? Don't you know we have been looking everywhere for you?"

"Why did you search for me?" Jesus answered. "Didn't you know I would be in my Father's house?"

They didn't understand his words at the time. But Mary often thought about them later. She knew her son was not an ordinary child.

Made for a Mission

Think
God gave me a very special mission to do here on Earth.

Remember
"I know the plans I have for you," announces the LORD. "I want you to enjoy success. I do not plan to harm you. I will give you hope for the years to come."
Jeremiah 29:11

Question
What do you want to do when you grow up? How do you think you can serve God through that job?

Formed for God's Family

Even before you were born, God planned for you to be part of his family. He wants you to know that Jesus is not only your King; he'll also be your brother. Just like you were born into your own family, by believing in Jesus, you can be "born again" into God's family. When we get baptized, we let others know we are part of God's family.

In this story, Jesus shows us that baptism is part of God's plan.

John Baptizes Jesus

MARK 1:1–10; JOHN 1:6–8, 15–34

God sent a man named John to prepare the way for Jesus. John lived in the desert and ate bugs and honey. He wore rough clothes made from camel's hair. But he had a very important message for the people: "Stop sinning and do good! Someone amazing is coming who is much greater than me."

Nearly all the people in the land came to listen to John and be baptized by him. Among the last to come was Jesus, the young carpenter from Nazareth. When John saw Jesus, God told him that this was the one who would save the people.

John said to Jesus, "Why are you coming to me? I need to be baptized by you!"

"This is what God wants," Jesus answered. "It is part of his plan."

131

Then John baptized Jesus as he had baptized all the others. When Jesus came up out of the water, John saw the sky open and the Holy Spirit come down upon Jesus like a dove. A voice from Heaven said, "This is my Son. I love him, and I am very pleased with him."

Then John told everyone that Jesus was the Son of God—the one God had promised to send to save the people.

Formed for God's Family

Think
God created me to be a part of his family.

Remember
"See what amazing love the Father has given us! Because of it, we are called children of God. And that's what we really are!"

1 John 3:1

Question
What kind of brother do you think Jesus is? What kind of brother or sister are you?

Being Like Jesus

As you grow up, God wants you to become like Jesus. That may sound pretty hard, but that's why God sends us the Holy Spirit. Jesus says the Holy Spirit is your friend, and he will help you know what to do and what to say. Becoming like Jesus means you learn to love other people the way God loves them.

Jesus chose the twelve disciples so he could teach them to become like him. He wants to do the same for you.

Day 23

Jesus Chooses Disciples

MATTHEW 4:18–22, 10:1–4; MARK 2:13–14, 3:13–19

Jesus was walking by the Sea of Galilee when he saw some men fishing. He called to them and told them they could become his followers. They were Andrew, Peter, James, and John. Some other men, Philip and Nathaniel, also became disciples.

One morning Jesus went by the place where the fishermen
were washing their nets to get ready to go fishing. Jesus stepped
into the boat that belonged to Andrew's brother, Peter. He asked
Andrew and Peter to push it out from the shore a little so that he
could talk to the people without being crowded. They did as he
asked, and from the fishing boat Jesus taught the people who sat
on the beach.

After he finished teaching, Jesus said to Peter, "Go out into the deep water and let down your nets."

"Teacher," said Peter, "we have fished all night and caught nothing. But if you say so, I will let down the net again."

When Peter obeyed Jesus, his net caught so many fish the men could not pull it up! There were so many fish the boat almost sank!

When Peter saw this, he was amazed at the power of God. He fell down at the feet of Jesus and said, "Lord, I am full of sin. I am not worthy of this. Please leave me."

But Jesus said to the men, "Don't be afraid! Follow me, and I will make you fishers of men."

Being Like Jesus

Think

God uses the Bible and the Holy Spirit to help me become like Jesus.

Remember

"But the fruit the Holy Spirit produces is love, joy and peace. It is being patient, kind and good. It is being faithful and gentle and having control of oneself."

Galatians 5:22–23

Question

Today's Bible verse describes several ways we can be like God. Which one do you need to work on the most?

It Takes Time

Do you sometimes get frustrated because you want to hurry and grow up? Do you want to get to do what grown-ups get to do? The thing is, God created you so that it takes time to grow up, so he isn't worried about how quickly you grow.

The same thing is true as we grow to become like Jesus. You can't rush it! God knows it takes time, and he knows that you have to take baby steps of faith, just like Peter in this story.

138

Peter's Faith Sinks

MATTHEW 14:22–33

After a busy day, Jesus needed some time alone. He told his disciples to get into their boat and row across the lake while he went up on a mountain to pray. But while Jesus was praying in the night, a great storm fell on the lake. From the mountain Jesus could see his disciples working hard to row against the waves.

Jesus decided to go to his disciples by walking on water. He walked right on top of the waves as if they were dry land!

The men in the boat saw a person coming toward them on the sea. They were afraid and cried out because they thought it must be a ghost. But Jesus called to them, "Don't be scared! It's me!" Then they saw it was their teacher.

Peter called to Jesus, "Lord, if it is really you, let me come to you on the water."

Jesus answered, "Come."

Peter leapt overboard, and he too walked on the water—until he noticed how big the waves had become.

He started to become afraid, and then he started to sink! "Lord, save me!" he cried.

Jesus reached out his hand and caught hold of Peter. He lifted Peter and helped him back into the boat. "Your faith is so small!" Jesus said. "Why didn't you believe me?"

The disciples were amazed. "You really are the Son of God!" they said.

It Takes Time

Think

Jesus knows I need to take baby steps as I grow to become like him.

Remember

"God began a good work in you. And I am sure that he will carry it on until it is completed."

Philippians 1:6

Question

What baby step can you take today to help you grow to become more like Jesus?

Thinking More of Others than Yourself

It's pretty easy to be selfish, but God wants us to think about other people more than we think about ourselves. He wants us to see other people who need help and try to do something about it. He wants us to see people who are hurt or sad or lonely and try to help them feel better.

Jesus was speaking to a crowd of people, and when it got close to dinnertime, he knew they were becoming hungry. There wasn't any place nearby to get food. Jesus didn't say, "Figure it out on your own." He looked at the people with compassion, and then he fed them.

Jesus Feeds 5,000

MATTHEW 14:13–21, MARK 6:30–44, LUKE 9:10–17

One day Jesus was teaching a huge crowd in an open and empty place. As it began to get late in the day, the disciples said to him, "There is nothing here for so many people to eat. Send them away before it is too late to get some food in town."

But Jesus replied, "They don't need to go away. You can give them food to eat."

That surprised the disciples. "Should we go into town to buy bread?" they asked. "We couldn't buy enough for each person here to have even one bite!"

"How many loaves do you have?" Jesus asked them.

One of the disciples found a young boy and brought him to Jesus. He said, "Here is a boy who has five barley loaves and two dried fish. But how far can that lunch go to feed such a large crowd?"

Jesus took the boy's five loaves and two fish in his hands. He looked up to Heaven and gave thanks for the food. Then he divided the loaves and the fish and gave the pieces to each of the disciples. The disciples walked among the people and handed out the bread and fish. They found they had enough food for everyone. They just kept breaking off pieces and breaking off pieces until everyone had eaten enough.

When everyone was full, there were still twelve baskets full of leftover bread and fish!

Thinking More of Others than Yourself

Think

God wants me to think less about myself and more about others.

Remember

"In everything, do to others what you would want them to do to you."

Matthew 7:12

Question

What do you sometimes have to do to find out what people need?

145

You Serve God by Serving Others

When you help someone, you're serving God. Sometimes God puts someone who needs help right in front of you. He is giving you a chance to be a servant. A servant does what needs to be done, no matter how big or small the job. Are you ready to jump in and help, without thinking about yourself? When you do that, you are God's servant!

Jesus told this story about how to love and serve others.

Day 26

The Good Samaritan

LUKE 10:25–37

Some people wanted Jesus to tell them more about how to follow God. Jesus said they should obey the commandment that says, "Love the Lord your God with all your heart and soul and strength and mind. And love your neighbor as you love yourself."

Then a curious man asked, "Who is my neighbor?"

146

Jesus answered by telling a story: "One day, a man was traveling down a road when some robbers attacked him. They took everything he had. They beat him up so badly they thought he was dead.

"A priest came down the same road, but when he saw the man lying there, he crossed to the other side and walked by. Later, a man who worked in the temple also came down the road. He passed by on the other side of the road, the same way the priest did.

"Then a man from Samaria came down the
road. He stopped as soon as he saw the hurt man.
He helped the man by putting ointment and
bandages on his wounds. Then he lifted the man
and put him on his own donkey.

"He took the man to an inn and cared for him all night. The next morning he gave money to the innkeeper and asked the innkeeper to take care of him until he got better."

Then Jesus said, "Which of these men do you think was a neighbor to the one who was robbed?"

The curious man answered, "The one who showed kindness."

"Yes," Jesus said. "Now you should go and do the same thing for others."

You Serve God by Serving Others

Think
I serve God by helping others.

Remember
"Anyone who wants to be important among you must be your servant."

Mark 10:43

Question
Where do you need to be on the lookout for ways to help others?

God Doesn't Give up on You

God will always welcome you home. He may be disappointed with something you've done, but he will always forgive you. He's ready to greet you with open arms and tell you how happy he is that you've come back to him.

Jesus told a story about a selfish son who runs away and wastes his father's money. When the son comes back, his father isn't angry with him. He is excited to see his son and welcomes him home.

Day 27

The Lost Son

LUKE 15:11–32

A parable is a story used to teach people about God. Jesus told this parable: A man had two sons. The younger son said to his father, "Give me the money that will be mine when you die. I want to use it now."

This made the father sad, but he did what his son asked. The younger son took his share of the money and left to live in a city far away.

But he wasn't careful or thoughtful with the money, and he quickly spent it all on foolish things. Soon, he had no money left!

So the younger son got a job taking care of some pigs. He was so hungry he wanted to eat the food the pigs were eating, but no one would let him. He started thinking about his father's house and how there was always plenty to eat there.

The son knew he had done a bad thing by spending all his money, so he decided to go back to his father. He thought, "Maybe he will let me be a servant."

While the son was still far down the road from his father's house, his father saw him coming. The man ran to his son and hugged him with joy.

"I am so sorry, Father," said the son. "I have done a bad thing, and I don't deserve to be called your son."

Before he could say any more, his father called to his servants, "Bring out the best robe. Let's have a party! My son was lost and now he's found!"

Jesus told this story to teach people that God feels the same way about his children. He never gives up on you!

God Doesn't Give Up on You

Think

God is my loving Father, and he will never give up on me.

Remember

"'This son of mine was dead. And now he is alive again. He was lost. And now he is found.' So they began to celebrate."

Luke 15:24

Question

Why does it make it easier to forgive someone when you think about how much God forgives you?

Lost and Found

It's easy to get lost when we choose to do what we want instead of doing what God tells us to do. Being lost can be really scary. But God doesn't want you to go your own way. He sent Jesus to find you and bring you back to him. You are part of God's family, and he wants you to be with him.

In this story, the shepherd doesn't wait for the missing sheep to come home. The shepherd knows the sheep is lost, and so he goes to find it.

Day 28

The Parable of the Lost Sheep

MATTHEW 18

Jesus told the people another story, this time about a lost sheep. "Imagine a shepherd has a hundred sheep," Jesus said, "but he loses one of them. Don't you think the shepherd would leave the ninety-nine other sheep and go look for the lost one? Wouldn't he search high and low for the lost sheep until he found it?"

159

The people in the crowd nodded their heads. A lot of them had sheep of their own, so they understood.

Then Jesus said, "Can you imagine how happy the shepherd will be when he finally finds his lost sheep? He would put the sheep over his shoulders and carry it home. He would tell all his friends and neighbors the good news. 'My sheep was lost,' he'd say. 'But now I've found it!'"

Jesus looked around and said, "This story shows how much your Father in Heaven cares for you. He is like that shepherd, and he does not want one single person to be lost."

Lost and Found

Think

I am part of God's family, and he wants me to be with him.

Question

What do you think God wants you to do when you realize you have gone your own way instead of God's way?

Remember

"The Son of Man came to look for the lost and save them."

Luke 19:10

God Sees You

God knows exactly where you are every minute of the day. He knew where you were an hour ago, and he knows where you will be tomorrow. God pays attention to you because he cares about you. It is one of the ways he says, "You matter to me. You are valuable."

Zacchaeus wanted to see Jesus, but he was very short and couldn't see over the crowd, so he climbed up a tree. But Jesus knew exactly where Zacchaeus was.

Jesus Goes to Zacchaeus' House

LUKE 19:1–10

Jesus was teaching and healing people, and a big crowd gathered around. A very short man named Zacchaeus really wanted to see Jesus, but he couldn't see over the people in front of him. Then he had an idea. He ran ahead of the crowd and climbed a sycamore tree beside the road. He waited there for Jesus and the others to pass by.

When Jesus got to the tree, he stopped walking. He looked up. Then he called out, "Zacchaeus, hurry and come down. Today I must visit your house!"

Zacchaeus was so happy! He came down at once and took Jesus to his house for a meal. Some people were angry that Jesus had decided to go to Zacchaeus' house because Zacchaeus was a tax collector. Sometimes Zacchaeus charged people too much money and then he kept it for himself. But when Zacchaeus understood how much Jesus loved him, his heart changed, and he wanted to help others.

Zacchaeus told Jesus, "I am going to give half my money to the poor. If I have taken anything from anyone, I will give back four times as much as I took."

Jesus said to him, "Today, salvation has come to this family."

God Sees You

Think
God pays attention to me because he loves me.

Remember
"He watches over those who put their hope in his faithful love."
Psalm 33:18

Question
Do I pay attention to others?

Jesus Is the Light of the World

Because of Jesus, the Light of the World, we are no longer in the dark. We don't have to wonder about who God is and what he is really like. The Bible says we see God when we look at Jesus. Jesus came to Earth so we could get to know God.

As Jesus rode into Jerusalem on the day we celebrate as Palm Sunday, the people rejoiced and praised him.

Day 30

Jesus Travels to Jerusalem

MATTHEW 21:1–11

Jesus needed to travel to the city of Jerusalem for the Passover feast. He sent his disciples to bring him a donkey. He knew his time on Earth was coming to an end.

As Jesus rode over the mountain toward Jerusalem, a huge crowd of people who had come to see Jesus threw clothes on the road in front of him. It looked like a giant colorful carpet leading into the city. They were so happy to see him that they welcomed him the way they would a king or a hero.

170

The crowd waved palm branches and shouted, "Blessed is the King who comes in the name of the Lord! May there be peace and glory in the highest Heaven!"

They said these things because they really believed Jesus was the Messiah, the King sent from God. They hoped that he would come into the city and set up a golden throne right then.

Jesus Is the Light of the World

Think
Jesus shows us what God is like.

Remember
"The Son is the exact likeness of God, who can't be seen."
Colossians 1:15

Question
What can you do to get to know Jesus better?

Thinking Like Jesus

Even though Jesus was the Son of God, he never thought he was too important to help others. He would do things for them, no matter how unimportant or unfair it seemed. And he served each person with all his heart. That's the way Jesus wants you to think about serving others. He wants you to follow his example.

Jesus and the disciples (his followers that he was close to) lived in a time when people needed to wash their feet when they came into a house. The roads were dusty, and many people wore sandals. Usually, the lowest ranking person in the house or a servant would wash everybody else's feet. It was considered a lowly job, but Jesus set an example for us by washing his friends' feet.

Jesus Serves His Friends

JOHN 13:1–17

Jesus and his disciples went to an upstairs room to celebrate the Passover feast. While his disciples were at the table, Jesus stood up and took off his outer robe. He tied a long towel around his waist, the same way that a servant would. Then, he poured water into a bowl and carried it,

172

kneeling near the feet of one of the disciples. When he began to wash the first disciple's feet, they were all surprised. Jesus went around to each of the disciples and washed their feet, just like he was a servant in the house.

When Jesus came to Peter, the disciple tried to stop Jesus. "No, Lord, don't wash my feet."

"If I don't wash you," Jesus said, "then you don't really belong to me."

"Okay, then," Peter said. "Don't just wash my feet. Wash my hands and my head too!"

Jesus told his friend, "A person who has taken a bath needs only to wash his feet. The rest of his body is clean. And you are clean."

Jesus looked around the room at his disciples and said, "Do you know what I have done for you? You call me 'Master' and 'Lord.' You are right. That is what I am. Now I, your Lord and Master, I have washed your feet. I have given you an example to follow.

"You should do as I have done and wash each other's feet."

Jesus wants us to help and serve each other. He wants us to think of others as important because Jesus loves them too.

Think

When I think like Jesus, I am happy to serve others.

Remember

."As you deal with one another, you should think and act as Jesus did."

Philippians 2:5

Question

What are the jobs you try to avoid that could be helpful to others?

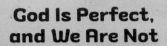

God Is Perfect, and We Are Not

Day 32

Nobody is perfect. There are some people who pretend they are perfect, but they are just like everybody else—they make mistakes too. But we can't hide our mistakes from God. We can't pretend we never mess up, because God sees what really happened. But here is the Good News: God doesn't expect you to be perfect. He knows you will make mistakes, and yet he still wants you to help him with his work here on Earth.

Peter wasn't perfect, but Jesus still chose him to be one of his disciples. In this story, when Jesus is arrested, Peter gets scared and lies to protect himself.

176

Peter Denies Jesus

MATTHEW 26:31–35, 69–74, LUKE 22:31–34, 54–62,
JOHN 18:15–27

On the night before Jesus died, he told his disciples, "Soon I am going away to a place where you cannot come right now. But when I have gone, remember to love one another just like I have loved you."

Peter said, "Lord, why can't I follow you now? I am ready to lay down my life for you!"

"Really?" Jesus asked. "The truth is, Peter, before the rooster crows tomorrow morning, you will say three times that you don't know me at all."

But Peter couldn't believe that! "Even if they try to kill me," he promised, "I will never tell people I don't know you."

Later that night, Jesus and his disciples went to a garden to pray. While they were there, Jesus was arrested. All the disciples were so afraid of the soldiers they ran away.

178

The soldiers and Jewish leaders brought Jesus to the high priest. Peter followed at a distance and waited outside the door. A servant girl saw him standing in the shadows. "Aren't you one of the men who follows Jesus?" she asked, staring at his face.

"No," said Peter, shaking his head.

It was cold that night. Peter sat in front of a fire to warm himself as he waited. Another person at the fire looked closely at Peter. "You were with Jesus, weren't you?" the man said.

Peter felt afraid. "No," he said. "I was never with him."

Later, another person pointed at Peter and said, "You must be a follower of Jesus. You have the same accent."

But Peter stood up and shouted, "I don't know what you're talking about! I don't know him!"

Just then, Peter heard the rooster crow. He realized that what Jesus said would happen had just come true. Peter had denied that he knew Jesus three times. Peter hung his head and cried.

God Is Perfect, and We Are Not

Think
God knows I'm not perfect, yet he still wants me to help him.

Remember
"My grace is all you need. My power is strongest when you are weak."
2 Corinthians 12:9

Question
How can you help God with his work?

God Wants You to Believe

Faith means you trust God even when you're not sure how things are going to end up. No matter what happens, God wants you to remember that he loves you and he has a special plan for you. God shows you that special plan when you follow Jesus. You can pray this prayer: "Jesus, I believe in you, and I believe that God sent you so I could join his family. I trust you to help me follow God's plan for my life."

This story shows us Jesus understood what it is like to trust God, even when things seem bad.

Day 33

God's Greatest Sacrifice

MATTHEW 27:32–54, 28:2–7; MARK 15:16–41,
LUKE 23:33–49, 24:1–2

The Roman governor decided that Jesus must die. Soldiers put Jesus on a cross and nailed him to it. Jesus prayed for them. He said, "Father, forgive them. They don't know what they're doing."

183

Soon a sudden darkness came over the land. It lasted for three hours. In the middle of the afternoon, after six hours of terrible pain on the cross, Jesus spoke his last words before dying: "It is finished! Father, I give my spirit into your hands!"

Then Jesus died. At the same moment, the heavy curtain of the temple that hid the holiest place was torn in two from top to bottom. The earth shook. Rocks split open.

When the Roman officer in charge of the soldiers saw what was happening, he said, "Surely this was the Son of God!"

God Wants You to Believe

Think

God wants me to trust him— on good days and bad days.

Remember

"Some people did accept him and did believe in his name. He gave them the right to become children of God."

John 1:12

Question

Why do you think we have bad days even when we follow Jesus?

187

Jesus Keeps His Promises

The Good News is that Jesus did exactly what he said he would do. He rose from the dead! He came back to life! That means three things: Jesus is who he said he was, he has the power he said he had, and he kept the promises he made. When the Son of God makes a promise, you can count on it!

Day 34

188

Jesus Rises from the Dead

MATTHEW 28:1–8

Some women walked to Jesus' tomb two days after his death. They brought sweet-smelling spices to put in his grave.

But when they came to the cave where Jesus was buried, they were surprised. Someone had rolled away the huge stone at the entrance. The tomb of Jesus was standing wide open!

The women did not know about the amazing thing that had happened before they got there. A great earthquake had shaken the ground and rocks. An angel had come down from Heaven and rolled the stone away. When the soldiers who were guarding the tomb saw the angel sitting on the stone with his bright face and shining robe, they fainted and fell to the ground.

The women looked in the tomb and saw that Jesus' body was gone. Then they saw two angels sitting at each end of the tomb!

The angels said, "Don't be afraid! You're looking for Jesus, but he's not here. He has risen from the dead! Go and tell the disciples. You will see Jesus again soon."

The women could hardly believe the good news! They ran quickly to tell the disciples.

Jesus Keeps His Promises

Think

Jesus told his disciples he would rise from the dead, and he did!

Remember

"I am the resurrection and the life. Anyone who believes in me will live, even if they die."

John 11:25

Question

Have you ever thanked Jesus for keeping his promises? What do you need to say to him today?

193

God Gives You Another Chance

There's nothing you could ever do to make God stop loving you. Even if you do something wrong, he still wants to hold you in his arms and tell you how much he loves you. No matter what you do, God's love for you will never end, and when you do something wrong, he will always give you another chance.

Remember when Peter said he didn't know Jesus? He said it three different times. In this Bible story, Jesus gives Peter another chance.

Jesus Gives Peter a New Task

JOHN 21:15–19

A few weeks after Jesus rose from the dead, he went down to the shore where the disciples were fishing. He served them a breakfast of bread and fish. After breakfast Jesus turned to Peter, the disciple who said three different times that he didn't know Jesus. Jesus asked, "Peter, do you love me?"

"Yes, Lord," Peter said. "You know that I love you."

Jesus said, "Feed my lambs."

After a while Jesus asked him again, "Peter, do you love me?"
Peter answered him like he did before: "Yes, Lord, you know that I love you."
This time Jesus said, "Take care of my sheep."
Jesus asked a third time, "Peter, do you love me?"

Peter didn't understand why Jesus had asked the question a third time. He answered, "Lord, you know everything. You know that I love you."

Jesus said, "Feed my sheep." And he added, "Follow me."

Peter said three different times that he didn't know Jesus. Now Jesus asked Peter three different times to say that he loved Jesus. Jesus gave Peter a second chance to do his work as a disciple.

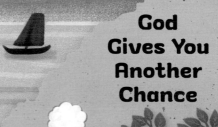

God Gives You Another Chance

Think
No matter what I do, God will always love me.

Remember
"God did not send his Son into the world to judge the world. He sent his Son to save the world through him."
John 3:17

Question
Because God gives you second chances, what do you think he wants you to do when other people mess up and need forgiveness?

197

Jesus Gives You a Mission

Jesus came to tell everyone that God loves them and he wants them to be part of his family. Now Jesus wants us to tell people the same thing. He wants us to help him tell people that God wants to be their Savior. This is a special mission that Jesus is passing on to you.

The Disciples Spread the Good News

MATTHEW 28:18–20, LUKE 24:46–53, JOHN 20:19–23, ACTS 1:7–11, 2:1–4

Jesus met his disciples on a mountain in Galilee. Many people came to see Jesus. He told them, "Go out and tell everyone in all nations about the good news of the Son of God. Baptize them and teach them the things I have taught you. Know that I am with you always."

198

Later Jesus appeared to his disciples in the city of Jerusalem. He told his followers that God would send down the gift of the Holy Spirit. He said, "When the Holy Spirit comes to you, you will have a new power. You will speak my name in Jerusalem, in Judea, in Samaria, and in the farthest parts of the earth."

The Jewish feast of Pentecost was ten days after Jesus went to Heaven. On that day the believers in Christ were together in an upstairs room. Suddenly they heard a sound from Heaven that was like the rushing of a mighty wind. They saw something that looked like tongues of fire over the head of each of them. Then the Spirit of God came on all the believers gathered there. They began to speak in languages they had not known before!

People from all over town came to see what was happening. When they did, they heard Jewish people speaking all the different languages that people in the city knew. The followers of Jesus were praising God and telling the Good News of Jesus in languages from all over the world.

Then Peter explained that God had given Jesus' followers a gift called the Holy Spirit. He told the crowd that Jesus had come to forgive their sins.

Many Jews believed and became followers of Jesus on that day. They told everyone they could about the Good News of Jesus.

Jesus Gives You a Mission

Think
Jesus wants me to tell people about God's love for them.

Remember
"I want to complete the work the Lord Jesus has given me. He wants me to tell others about the good news of God's grace."

Acts 20:24

Question
How can you help others become friends with God?

Heaven, Your Real Home

Do you know that God wants you to come and live with him in Heaven forever? Even though there are lots of great things here on Earth, Heaven will be even better. Jesus is getting things ready for you right now, but while you're here on Earth, he wants you to learn how to love him and love other people. You show your love for Jesus by helping others.

Day 37

Jesus Will Come Back Again

MATTHEW 25:31–40, 1 THESSALONIANS 4:16–17

Jesus told the people that one day he would come back to Earth with all his angels. When that happens, Jesus will sit on a throne, and people from all over the world will stand before him. He will separate the people into two groups, like a shepherd who separates the sheep from the goats.

206

King Jesus will say to the people on his right, "Come with me into the Kingdom. When I was hungry, you fed me. When I was thirsty, you gave me something to drink. When I was sick, you took care of me."

Then those people on his right will ask, "Lord, when did we do those things for you? We don't remember feeding you or caring for you."

King Jesus will say, "Anything you did for a poor brother or sister, you did for me."

Then King Jesus will turn to those on his left. "Now you people must leave. I was hungry, and you didn't feed me. I was thirsty, and you didn't share your water. I was sick, and you did not care for me."

The people on his left will cry out, "Lord, what are you talking about? When did these things happen? When did we leave you hungry or sick?"

King Jesus will say, "Whenever you did not care for a hurting brother or sister, you also did not care for me."

Heaven, Your Real Home

Think
When I help others, I show Jesus I love him.

Remember
"Anything you did for one of the least important of these brothers and sisters of mine, you did for me."
Matthew 25:40

Question
What are some ways you can help others?

207

The Power of God's Word

God's Word is not like any other. It is truth! When God speaks, things change. God's Word causes miracles. It transforms people, releases power, heals, and brings things to life. In fact, everything around you—all of creation—exists because God spoke.

When Jesus spoke to Saul, his life was never the same again.

Saul Sees the Light

ACTS 8:1–3, 9:1–22

Many people believed that Jesus was the Messiah. But a man named Saul thought the Christians were telling lies. He wanted to stop them. He put them in jail and even had some believers killed. But it didn't stop the Christians from being joyful and telling everyone how Jesus had changed their lives.

One day, as Saul was traveling down the road, a bright light flashed from Heaven. It was brighter than the sun and blinded Saul's eyes. He fell to the ground. Then a voice called, "Saul, Saul, why are you fighting against me?"

Saul asked, "Who are you, Lord?"

"I am Jesus," said the voice. "I am the one you are trying to stop. Get up and go into the city. You will be told what to do."

Saul opened his eyes, but he couldn't see. He was blind. His friends had to lead him to a house where he could rest. Saul sat in the darkness praying to God with all his heart.

A believer named Ananias lived in the city. God spoke to
Ananias and told him to go to Saul. "Lay your hands on him, and
give him back his sight," God said.

Ananias was surprised and said, "God, I have heard about all
the bad things Saul has done. He arrests anyone who follows you.
Do you really want me to go see him?"

But God said, "Go. I have chosen Saul to take my name to
people around the world."

Ananias obeyed. He found the house that Saul was in and laid his hands on Saul's head. He said, "Brother Saul, the Lord Jesus sent me so that you may have your sight and be filled with the Holy Spirit. Don't wait any more. Get up, and be baptized."

Then something like scales fell off Saul's eyes, and he could see. From then on Saul told people near and far about the love and power of Jesus. Everyone who heard him was amazed. You may know Saul by his second name: Paul.

The Power of God's Word

Think
The Bible is God's Word.

Remember
"'If you obey my teaching,' he said, 'you are really my disciples. Then you will know the truth. And the truth will set you free.'"
John 8:31–32

Question
Why should you spend time reading God's Word, the Bible?

213

God Cares for the Whole World

Day 39

God wants friends from every nation he created, and he wants us to help them find him. Some people do this by traveling to other countries and sharing God's message. But there's another way you can help: by praying for the world. Prayer connects you with people wherever they are, near or far. You can pray for someone whether they are ten feet or 10,000 miles away!

In this Bible story, an angel tells Philip to go to a distant town to find a new friend for God.

The Man in the Chariot

ACTS 8:25–40

The disciples traveled all over the land telling people about Jesus. One day, the disciple Philip was walking down the road when he saw a chariot pulled by horses. An African man from Ethiopia was sitting in it, reading a scroll.

As the chariot came closer, God's Holy Spirit said to Philip, "Go stand close to the chariot."

Philip obeyed. He saw that the scroll contained the words of the prophet Isaiah. Philip asked the man, "Do you understand what you're reading?"

214

The Ethiopian answered, "How can I understand it unless someone explains it to me? Can you? If you can, come up into the chariot and sit with me."

So Philip did. The Ethiopian was reading these words of Isaiah:

He was led like a sheep to be killed. Just as lambs are silent while their wool is being cut off, he did not open his mouth.

The man asked Philip, "Tell me, please. Who is the prophet talking about?"

Philip knew these words were about Jesus. He told the Ethiopian man all about the Good News of Jesus Christ. The man opened his heart and believed in Jesus. They were near some water, so Philip baptized the Ethiopian man right then and there!

God Cares for the Whole World

Think
I can help God by praying for a different country every day.

Remember
"Go into all the world. Preach the good news to everyone."
Mark 16:15

Question
What will help you remember to take time every day to pray for the world?

Made to Last Forever

God made you to last forever. He designed you to be like him, to live for eternity. One day we will all stand before the throne of God, thanking and praising him. Together we will say to God:

"You are worthy, our Lord and God!"

Forever Home

REVELATION 7:9–17; 21

The apostle John had a vision about Heaven. He saw the throne of God and a huge crowd of people wearing white robes gathered in front of it. They were waving palm branches and calling out, "Salvation belongs to our God, who sits on the throne. Salvation also belongs to the Lamb."

All the angels were standing around God's throne, and there were some others there called elders. One of the elders told John about the people in white: "They will never be hungry or thirsty again. The Lamb of God will be their shepherd forever."

Then the elder told John the best part: "And God will wipe away every tear from their eyes." In Heaven there will be no more crying. There will be no more pain. God is going to make everything brand new.

221

John saw a beautiful city coming down from Heaven, shining with the glory of God. It had a huge, high wall with twelve gates made of pearl, and there was an angel at every gate. The city was made of gold so pure it looked like glass. It didn't even need the sun or the moon to shine on it, because God's glory provided all the light.

The gates of the city will never be shut. And people from every nation will walk in the light of the city.

An angel said to John, "You can trust these words. They are true."

Made to Last Forever

Think
God made me to last forever!

Remember
"Whoever does what God wants them to do lives forever."
1 John 2:17

Question
Think about how much God must love you if he wants to be with you forever. Pray and thank him for letting you live forever with him in Heaven.